Mastering the Art of Trading:
A Comprehensive Guide

Michael R. Taylor

Acknowledgment

I would like to express my heartfelt gratitude to everyone who contributed to the creation of this book.

A special thank you to my family and friends for their love, encouragement, and understanding during the long hours spent immersed in writing. Your unwavering belief in me and your patience through the ups and downs of this creative endeavor mean more to me than words can express.

I am indebted to the countless individuals who inspired and influenced me along the way, from mentors and teachers to fellow writers and artists. Your wisdom, creativity, and generosity have left an indelible mark on my journey as an author.

Last but certainly not least, I extend my deepest gratitude to you, dear reader, for your interest in this book. Your curiosity, passion, and support are the driving force behind every word written, and it is my sincere hope that this book brings you joy, inspiration, and a sense of connection.

With heartfelt thanks,

Copyright © 2024 by Michael R. Taylor

All rights reserved. No part of this publication may be reproduced, distributed, or transmitted in any form or by any means, including photocopying, recording, or other electronic or mechanical methods, without the prior written permission of the publisher, except in the case of brief quotations embodied in critical reviews and certain other noncommercial uses permitted by copyright law.

Content

Chapter	Page
Introduction	11
Getting Started with Trading	14
Basics of Technical Analysis	19
Fundamental Analysis	26
Risk Management	30
Developing a Trading Strategy	35
Psychology of Trading	39
Advanced Trading Strategies	45
Day Trading vs. Swing Trading	49
Cryptocurrency Trading Insights	53
Leveraging Technology in Trading	56
Long-Term Investing Strategies	60
Trading in Volatile Markets	64
Building a Diverse Portfolio	67
Conclusion	79

Introduction

Within the expansive and ever-changing arena of finance, the art of trading shines as a light of opportunity amidst the turbulent waves of the market. "Mastering the Art of Trading: A Comprehensive Guide" acts as your reliable compass, directing you through the complex paths of the financial markets with both a high level of expertise and a high level of dexterity.

This book, which was crafted with painstaking attention to detail, is designed to accommodate traders of all levels of expertise, from novices who are just beginning their journey into the world of trading to seasoned pros who are perfecting their techniques to adapt to the always shifting market landscape.

You will go on a journey that is filled with insightful analysis, pragmatic insights, and actionable techniques, each of which has been thoughtfully crafted to provide you with the required armoury to survive in the competitive field of trading. This adventure will take place inside the constraints of nearly 500 pages that are illuminating. Each chapter contains a wealth of information that is just waiting to be discovered by you. From the intricacies of market dynamics to the realms of technical and fundamental analysis, from the development of robust risk management strategies to the utilisation of the profound impact of psychology in trading decisions, each chapter is a treasure trove of information.

Whether you are interested in the rapid manoeuvres of day trading, the calculated swings of swing trading, the complexity of options and futures, or the mysterious realm of cryptocurrency trading, this compendium is your thorough reference to all of these topics. By maintaining a consistent concentration on both short-term gains and the persistent pursuit of long-term wealth building, you will acquire the knowledge necessary to construct a diversified portfolio that is capable of withstanding the most intense market storms.

Before beginning the journey, it is necessary to have a fundamental grasp of the heartbeat of the market. This involves examining the market's complexities and intricacies in order to reveal the fundamental principles that control its ebbs and flows. With this core information in hand, you will venture into the world of technical analysis, where you will learn how to master the art of analysing charts, patterns, and indicators in order to get insights into market trends and prospective opportunities.

Nevertheless, trading is not only a science; rather, it is a complex dance that involves both intellectual analysis and the psyche of individuals. In this way, you will go on a comprehensive examination of the human psychology, finding the cognitive mistakes, emotions, and prejudices that frequently obscure judgement and cause trading techniques to fail. You will learn to tame the wild horse of human emotion by engaging in self-reflection and practicing self-discipline. You will learn to use it as a tool for making well-informed decisions rather than giving in to the vagaries of human emotion at random.

This book explores risk management in great detail, leaving no stone unturned in its investigation of this essential facet of trading. Risk management is the cornerstone of any successful trading enterprise. Through the use of stop-loss methods and position sizing, you will acquire the knowledge and skills necessary to navigate the perilous waters of risk with poise and accuracy, ensuring that each trade is a calculated step towards achieving your financial objectives.

This book will provide you with a plethora of practical tactics and approaches, each of which is designed to empower you in your trading adventure. As you continue through the pages, you will come across these items. You will investigate a wide variety of strategies, ranging from arbitrage to trend following, momentum trading to value investing, and everything in between. Each of these strategies presents its own distinct set of opportunities and obstacles.

There is, however, a more profound goal that extends beyond the simple accumulation of wealth; this drive is for mastery, for self-discovery, and for fulfilment. A voyage of human development and enlightenment, trading is not only a means to an end but rather a journey in and of itself. Self-control, resiliency, and an unyielding dedication to the pursuit of continuous development are all necessary components. And as you make your way through the winding roads of the market, you will come to realise that the greatest rewards are not measured solely in terms of monetary value, but rather in the profound sense of purpose and accomplishment that comes from being an expert in the art of trading.

Consequently, regardless of whether you are a rookie trader who is about to embark on your first voyage or an experienced veteran who is exploring new regions, "Mastering the Art of Trading" will serve as your trustworthy companion, shedding light on the way forward and enabling you to capture the numerous possibilities that are poised to present themselves in the near future. You will go on a voyage of transformation, exceeding the bounds of the ordinary in order to attain amazing success in the exciting world of trading. You will utilise knowledge as your guide and perseverance as your compass as you make your way through this adventure.

Chapter 1: Understanding Market Dynamics

In order to successfully navigate the complex landscape of trading, it is absolutely necessary to have a comprehensive understanding of the dynamics of the market. Markets, which are analogous to complex ecosystems, are susceptible to the effect of a wide variety of factors, which include economic indicators, geopolitical events, and investor sentiment, amongst others. The purpose of this chapter is to begin on a quest to untangle the intricate web of market dynamics. We will investigate how each element intertwines to determine market movements, as well as how traders can use this insight to their advantage.

Indicators of the economy serve as the foundation upon which financial market behaviour is built. These essential indicators of an economy, such as the growth of the gross domestic product (GDP), the unemployment rate, and inflation, act as guiding lights that shed light on the course that asset prices take. Through the process of immersing themselves in the world of economic data and recognising the implications that these indicators have on the market, traders are able to make informed judgements that allow them to navigate the stormy seas with accuracy.

The growth in gross domestic product, which is sometimes heralded as the barometer of economic health, has a significant impact on the sentiment of the market. Strong growth in the gross domestic product (GDP) is indicative of a thriving economy, which instills confidence among investors and drives commodity prices higher. On the other hand, sluggish growth or contraction can inspire fear and uncertainty, which can lead to market downturns. Trading professionals who are interested in profiting from these changes pay close attention to GDP figures and seize opportunities when they present themselves.

The rates of unemployment, which are another important economic indicator, provide vital insights on the realities of the unemployment market. There is a possibility that high unemployment rates are an indication of economic distress, which can discourage consumer purchasing and decrease market sentiment. A decrease in the unemployment rate, on the other hand, may be an indication of an expansion of the economy, which would inspire confidence and drive asset prices upward. Traders who are in tune with the pulse of employment statistics are able to predict market reactions and alter their methods accordingly in order to ride the wave of market movements.

The dynamics of the market are significantly impacted by inflation, which is a force that operates in the background without being noticed. Generally speaking, moderate inflation is considered to be an indication of a strong economy because it is suggestive of increased demand and rising salaries. Nevertheless, excessive inflation can bring about a decline in purchasing power, which in turn can shake investor confidence and bring about market corrections. Individuals who are skilled in the interpretation of inflationary trends are able to position themselves strategically, so protecting themselves from inflationary pressures and capturing chances despite the volatility of the market.

In the context of global markets, geopolitical events have the potential to act as powerful catalysts, capable of sparking fires of uncertainty and stirring up upheaval. Shockwaves are sent across the financial markets as a result of wars, terrorist attacks, and political upheavals. These wave-like phenomena cause dramatic variations in the pricing of assets. To successfully navigate the perilous landscape of geopolitical risk, traders need to maintain a state of vigilance and demonstrate agility and insight.

Gold and government bonds are examples of safe-haven assets

that frequently appear as havens of stability during times of global instability. These assets attract investors who are risk-averse and are looking for sanctuary from the volatility of the market. On the other hand, assets that are directly linked to countries or industries that are directly touched by geopolitical events may face increased volatility. This presents traders with both dangers and opportunities. It is possible for traders to navigate turbulent seas with confidence, so minimising risk and maximising returns, if they keep themselves informed of events in global affairs and evaluate the significance of these developments on the market.

The emotion of investors acts as the "invisible hand" that guides market trends and shapes the ebb and flow of asset prices. The emotion of the market is collectively influenced by news headlines, the buzz on social media, and the behaviour of institutional investors. This collective influence drives herd behaviour and shapes market dynamics. Traders who are skilled at interpreting investor emotions are able to identify market trends before they become realised, putting themselves in a strategic position to capitalise on opportunities that are just entering the market.

In point of fact, adaptability is of the utmost importance in the world of trade. The dynamics of the market are always evolving, and they are driven by a multitude of factors that are impossible to foresee with complete confidence. As traders, the ability to adjust to shifting circumstances and to adjust our plans in reaction to developing events is what differentiates those who are successful from those who are only hopeful.

Despite their immense value, economic indicators are not foolproof when it comes to predicting the behaviour of the market. Inaccuracies in the data, unexpected revisions, or unexpected shocks from the outside world have the potential to derail even the most precisely set out trading strategy. Therefore, while we pay attention to the direction that is provided by economic data, we must also maintain vigilance and be sensitive to the subtleties of the market's rhythm that is constantly shifting.

The nature of geopolitical events is such that they are subject to unpredictability. There are some that can be anticipated to a certain extent; yet, the timing and magnitude of their impact on the market frequently contradict common thinking. Trading professionals are required to cultivate a high awareness of geopolitical developments by watching global news outlets and geopolitical risk indexes in order to assess the potential dangers and opportunities that may arise.

Additionally, the sentiment of investors is a blade with two edges. When it comes to market trends and probable reversals, it can provide significant insights; nevertheless, it is also subject to unreasonable enthusiasm or unwarranted pessimism depending on the circumstances. It is imperative that traders exercise prudence, avoiding the temptation to mindlessly follow the crowd and instead depend on their own research and judgement.

Furthermore, in order to be successful in trading, one must possess not only a profound comprehension of the dynamics of the market, but also the qualities of discipline, patience, and emotional endurance. Perhaps the most undervalued yet crucial talent of all is the capacity to maintain composure and calmness in the face of adversity, to adhere to one's trading plan even when the market appears set on testing one's resolve, and to remain calm and collected in challenging circumstances.

As we go out on this adventure into the core of market dynamics, let us not overlook the significance of lifelong education and the pursuit of personal growth. A never-ending classroom, the markets teach lessons in humility, perseverance, and flexibility to those who are willing to learn them. It is possible for us to improve our trading abilities and become more successful if we are willing to take on the obstacles that they provide and grow from the experiences that we have.

In the chapters that are to come, we are going to go even further into the complexities of market analysis, risk management, and trading psychology. We are going to investigate a wide range of trading strategies and methods, analysing their advantages and disadvantages, and determining the circumstances in which they are most successful. We will also, and perhaps most significantly, reflect on the lessons that we have learned from both our triumphs and our disappointments, with the goal of refining our approach and aiming for mastery in the ever-changing world of trading.

In light of this, let us go on this adventure together, armed with knowledge, wisdom, and a fair dose of humility. Because in the world of financial markets, where everything is unpredictable, the only thing that is guaranteed is uncertainty. However, if we are diligent, persistent, and willing to adjust to changing circumstances, we will be able to successfully traverse these uncharted seas and emerge victorious.

Chapter 2: Designing a Robust Trading Strategy

Beginning a trip into the world of trading necessitates the creation of a solid road map, one that expertly navigates the complexities of the market while maintaining a resilient and resilient mindset. This chapter marks the beginning of the painstaking process of developing a comprehensive trading strategy that is personalised to your specific trading persona, ambitions, and level of comfort with risk.

Establishing Your Goals and Objectives

At the beginning of any trade endeavour, it is of the utmost importance to have a clear purpose. What are your goals in regard to your finances? Are you looking for financial benefits in the short term to supplement your income, or are you striving for the steady building of wealth over the course of a longer period of time? The process of defining your objectives not only serves to offer you with guidance, but it also acts as the foundation around which your entire strategy is constructed.

The Process of Selecting Your Trading Style

Once your goals have been outlined, the next incredibly important step is to choose a trading style that is congruent with your personality and the way you live your life. When it comes to trading, do you have a preference for the fast-paced environment of day trading, in which positions are opened and closed within the span of a single trading day? Alternately, does the possibility of maintaining positions for a number of days or weeks, as in swing trading, better correspond with your preferences? The day trading style is characterised by its intense intensity, which is powered by adrenaline, whereas swing trading requires patience and discipline. Each trading style has its own unique subtleties. It is of the utmost importance to select a fashion that not only complements your individuality but also fits in with your schedule and how much time you have available.

In the process of developing entry and exit rules

The subsequent phase involves the establishment of specific rules that regulate the beginning and ending of trades. This comes after the objectives have been established and the trading style has been selected. When you are in the thick of the turbulent waters of the market, these principles will serve as your guiding light, protecting you from making rash judgements that are motivated by your emotions. Your trading strategy will benefit from the structure and discipline that these principles introduce, regardless of whether they are based on fundamental analysis, price action patterns, or technical indicators. In order to protect profits or minimise losses, they determine when to enter a transaction, at what price, and most importantly, when to abandon the trade. Maintaining a consistent adherence to these guidelines will help you develop a mindset that is conducive to making systematic decisions, which is necessary for sustained success in trading.

The process of putting risk management strategies into action There is no such thing as a complete trading plan that does not include robust risk management methods. Risk management is the foundation upon which the preservation of capital and one's ability to remain competitive in the market are established. It involves a wide range of techniques, such as assessing the proper amount of capital to risk on each trade and setting stop-loss orders to reduce the likelihood of incurring losses. The dispersion of risk and protection against adverse fluctuations in any one market are two benefits that come from diversifying your portfolio across several asset classes. This further strengthens your portfolio's defences against market volatility. If you manage risk in a smart manner, you can protect yourself from suffering catastrophic losses and increase your money in a way that is sustainable over time.

Continuous monitoring and adjustment are both required. Due to the ever-changing nature of financial markets, it is necessary to make a commitment to conducting continual monitoring and making adjustments. In order to stay adaptable and flexible, your trading strategy needs to be able to adapt to changing market dynamics and emerging trends. On a regular basis, evaluate your performance in comparison to the metrics that have been specified, recognising both your strong and weak points. Maintain a mindset that is receptive to the possibility of improving your plan, adding fresh insights, and altering parameters as the market conditions require. The ability to remain ahead of the curve and capitalise on new possibilities is a fundamental characteristic of great traders. Flexibility and flexibility are crucial traits that distinguish successful traders.

The Finalisation

The process of developing a robust trading strategy is a laborious endeavour that requires careful consideration of objectives, trading style, risk management, and flexibility. Nevertheless, those who follow this route with diligence will be rewarded with significant benefits. You may prepare the road for success in the ever-changing world of trading by creating clear objectives, choosing a trading style that is compatible with your goals, establishing disciplined entry and exit criteria, adopting rigorous risk management, and keeping alert in monitoring and adapting to changing circumstances.

Chapter 2: Designing a Robust Trading Strategy

Despite the fact that the route may be challenging, the destination, which is the ability to realise your goals and become financially independent, is what makes the journey worthwhile.

Beginning a trip into the world of trading necessitates the creation of a solid road map, one that expertly navigates the complexities of the market while maintaining a resilient and resilient mindset. This chapter marks the beginning of the painstaking process of developing a comprehensive trading strategy that is personalised to your specific trading persona, ambitions, and level of comfort with risk.

Establishing Your Goals and Objectives

At the beginning of any trade endeavour, it is of the utmost importance to have a clear purpose. What are your goals in regard to your finances? Are you looking for financial benefits in the short term to supplement your income, or are you striving for the steady building of wealth over the course of a longer period of time? The process of defining your objectives not only serves to offer you with guidance, but it also acts as the foundation around which your entire strategy is constructed.

The Process of Selecting Your Trading Style

Once your goals have been outlined, the next incredibly important step is to choose a trading style that is congruent with your personality and the way you live your life. When it comes to trading, do you have a preference for the fast-paced environment of day trading, in which positions are opened and closed within the span of a single trading day? Alternately, does the possibility of maintaining positions for a number of days or weeks, as in swing trading, better correspond with your preferences? The day trading style is characterised by its intense intensity, which is powered by adrenaline, whereas swing trading requires patience and discipline. Each trading style has its own unique subtleties. It is of the utmost importance to select a fashion that not only complements your individuality but also fits in with your schedule and how much time you have available.

In the process of developing entry and exit rules

The subsequent phase involves the establishment of specific rules that regulate the beginning and ending of trades. This comes after the objectives have been established and the trading style has been selected. When you are in the thick of the turbulent waters of the market, these principles will serve as your guiding light, protecting you from making rash judgements that are motivated by your emotions. Your trading strategy will benefit from the structure and discipline that these principles introduce, regardless of whether they are based on fundamental analysis, price action patterns, or technical indicators. In order to protect profits or minimise losses, they determine when to enter a transaction, at what price, and most importantly, when to abandon the trade. Maintaining a consistent adherence to these guidelines will help you develop a mindset that is conducive to making systematic decisions, which is necessary for sustained success in trading.

The process of putting risk management strategies into action

There is no such thing as a complete trading plan that does not include robust risk management methods. Risk management is the foundation upon which the preservation of capital and one's ability to remain competitive in the market are established. It involves a wide range of techniques, such as assessing the proper amount of capital to risk on each trade and setting stop-loss orders to reduce the likelihood of incurring losses. The dispersion of risk and protection against adverse fluctuations in any one market are two benefits that come from diversifying your portfolio across several asset classes. This further strengthens your portfolio's defences against market volatility. If you manage risk in a smart manner, you can protect yourself from suffering catastrophic losses and increase your money in a way that is sustainable over time.

Continuous monitoring and adjustment are both required. Due to the ever-changing nature of financial markets, it is necessary to make a commitment to conducting continual monitoring and making adjustments. In order to stay adaptable and flexible, your trading strategy needs to be able to adapt to changing market dynamics and emerging trends. On a regular basis, evaluate your performance in comparison to the metrics that have been specified, recognising both your strong and weak points. Maintain a mindset that is receptive to the possibility of improving your plan, adding fresh insights, and altering parameters as the market conditions require. The ability to remain ahead of the curve and capitalise on new possibilities is a fundamental characteristic of great traders. Flexibility and flexibility are crucial traits that distinguish successful traders.

conclusion

The process of developing a robust trading strategy is a laborious endeavour that requires careful consideration of objectives, trading style, risk management, and flexibility. Nevertheless, those who follow this route with diligence will be rewarded with significant benefits. You may prepare the road for success in the ever-changing world of trading by creating clear objectives, choosing a trading style that is compatible with your goals, establishing disciplined entry and exit criteria, adopting rigorous risk management, and keeping alert in monitoring and adapting to changing circumstances. It is important to remember that even though the road may be challenging, the destination, which is the attainment of your goals and financial freedom, makes every step worthwhile.Each and every step is important.

Chapter 3: Technical Analysis Techniques

Technical analysis is the foundation of trading since it provides traders with a comprehensive arsenal that allows them to interpret market patterns and anticipate probable price moves. Within the scope of this chapter, we look into the many technical analysis approaches that traders typically apply and investigate the ways in which these methodologies improve trading decisions.

Charts are the fundamental component of technical analysis. These charts provide a graphical representation of price data and reveal patterns that can be used to enhance trading methods. Candlestick charts, line charts, and bar charts are the most powerful forms of charts that traders use. There are many other types of charts as well. Traders are able to recognise trends, define support and resistance levels, and detect potential reversal patterns with the use of these charts, which display price movements over predetermined time periods.

Within the realm of technical analysis, support and resistance levels are considered to be essential structures because they define the thresholds at which the price interacts with temporary barriers. Support levels, which serve as floors, prevent further price declines, whilst resistance levels, which serve as ceilings, prevent further price increases from occurring. When traders are able to identify these levels on a chart, they are able to anticipate probable price swings and adjust their trading strategies accordingly.

Within the realm of technical analysis, indicators are an additional instrument that is indispensable. These indicators include mathematical computations that are based on price and volume data. Moving averages, oscillators, and trend-following indicators are examples of indicators that are widely used. The use of these instruments provides traders with assistance in recognising overbought or oversold conditions, determining the direction of trends, and determining the most appropriate entry and exit points for investments.

In addition to charts and indicators, pattern identification approaches are included in the scope of technical analysis. Traders are able to gain significant insights into future price movements by utilising chart patterns such as triangles, flags, and head and shoulders formations. Traders are able to predict future breakout or breakdown scenarios and position themselves advantageously in the market if they acquire the skill to locate these patterns and become proficient in their identification.

The ability of technical analysis to provide traders with useful insights into the dynamics of the market and probable price movements is the overriding philosophy that characterises this type of analysis. Chart analysis, support and resistance levels, indicators, and pattern recognition are all examples of techniques that traders may master to improve their trading decisions and increase their chances of being successful in the markets. Traders can improve their chances of success by understanding these strategies.
In addition, traders are provided with the capacity to respond to changing market conditions and to make judgements based on accurate information in real time through the utilisation of technical analysis. A dynamic approach to analysis allows traders to alter their tactics in response to developing trends and shifting price dynamics. This allows traders to make more informed decisions.

The adaptability of technical analysis to a wide range of asset classes and financial markets is one of the most significant advantages of this investment strategy. Regardless matter whether one is trading equities, currencies, commodities, or cryptocurrencies, the fundamentals of technical analysis continue to be applicable. As a result of this universality, traders are able to exploit their expertise across a variety of marketplaces, which significantly increases the number of trading opportunities available to them and diversifies their portfolios.

In addition to this, technical analysis is an extremely helpful instrument for using in risk management. It is possible for traders to place stop-loss orders in order to limit prospective losses and safeguard their capital. This is accomplished by identifying critical support and resistance levels. Furthermore, technical indicators can assist traders in evaluating the strength of a trend and determining the ideal entry and exit positions, which allows them to minimise risks and maximise possible earnings consequently maximising potential profits.

One further facet that should be brought to your attention is the psychological component of technical analysis. Participants in the market frequently engage in herd behaviour, which results in price fluctuations that are influenced by particular patterns and trends. Traders are able to capitalise on these psychological tendencies through the use of technical analysis, which identifies patterns and trends that are influenced by market emotion. By gaining a grasp of the psychological factors that influence price fluctuations, traders are able to anticipate the reactions of the market and make judgements that are influenced by probabilities rather than emotions.

In conclusion, technical analysis is a powerful instrument that gives traders significant insights into market trends and prospective price moves. Traders can benefit from this insightful information. It is possible for traders to improve their decision-making process, effectively manage risks, and increase their overall trading success if they learn the concepts of technical analysis and incorporate them into their trading strategies. Technical analysis continues to be an essential component of the trading landscape due to its adaptability, universality, and capacity to comprehend the psychological aspects of the market.

Chapter 4: Mastering Fundamental Analysis

By providing traders with a comprehensive perspective of the factors that are driving market dynamics, fundamental analysis serves as the foundation upon which intelligent trading decisions are built. basic research dives deeper into the basic elements that are driving market movements. These fundamental factors include economic data, corporate financials, and geopolitical events. Technical analysis, on the other hand, examines price actions and chart patterns. At the beginning of this chapter, we will set out on an adventure to discover the fundamentals of fundamental analysis and the essential role that it plays in the formation of trading methods.

One of the most important aspects of fundamental analysis is economic analysis, which places a significant emphasis on the value of macroeconomic data. When trying to get a sense of the state of the economy, traders carefully analyse several indicators such as the growth of the GDP, inflation rates, and interest rates. When traders have a comprehensive understanding of the economic landscape, they are better equipped to forecast the influence that economic changes will have on asset values. For example, a solid expansion in GDP combined with low inflation may be indicative of a healthy economy, which may in turn boost investor confidence and lead to an increase in stock prices. In the opposite direction, a rise in inflation rates that is accompanied by a slowdown in GDP growth may indicate that economic headwinds are there, which would cause investors to adopt a cautious approach. It is possible for traders to skillfully calibrate their trading tactics in accordance with the prevalent economic trends if they take the time to process economic insights.

In addition to economic analysis, corporate analysis is a fundamental component of fundamental analysis. This is especially true for traders who are primarily concerned with specific stocks inside the market. Obtaining essential insights into a company's financial health and growth potential can be accomplished by carefully examining the company's financial statements, earnings reports, and trends in the industry. When attempting to determine the true value of a company, experienced traders carefully examine many financial parameters, including the growth of sales, the margins of profit, and the levels of debt. The ability to recognise undervalued companies that are loaded with growth potential or overvalued stocks that are on the verge of performing a correction gives traders the ability to make intelligent judgements regarding their investments. Furthermore, by delving into the dynamics of the business and the competitive landscapes, traders are able to identify possibilities and risks that are peculiar to the sector, which helps to create a well-rounded approach to investment.

In addition to conducting economic and company analysis, skilled traders continue to keep a keen awareness of geopolitical developments and the repercussions those events have on global markets. The importance of maintaining a global awareness cannot be overstated, since the potential for seismic movements in asset prices can be unleashed by wars, political upheavals, and trade conflicts. It is possible that the escalation of geopolitical tensions may cause a dosage of volatility to be introduced into the financial markets, which will drive investors to readjust their risk exposures. Traders are able to make proactive adjustments to their trading tactics and successfully navigate through choppy market waters if they keep a close eye on geopolitical developments and the ripple effects they have.

There is a powerful arsenal in the toolkit of a trader that is comprised of fundamental and technical analysis working together in harmony. This arsenal provides traders with a diverse perspective on the dynamics of the market. Although fundamental research provides traders with a comprehensive understanding of the factors that are driving market movements, technical analysis provides traders with the ability to precisely time when they should enter and exit the market. By combining fundamental insights with technical indications, traders are given the ability to triangulate their trading decisions, which in turn strengthens their market savvy. In the process of beginning their journey to become fundamental analysis experts, it is absolutely necessary for traders to have a solid framework for doing research and analysis. To help you strengthen your skills in fundamental analysis, here are some important measures to take:

The first step is to define your investment universe. In order to determine the extent of your investigation, you need first identify the asset classes, markets, and sectors that you intend to concentrate on. Establishing a clear definition of your investment universe lays the framework for conducting targeted research, regardless of whether you are investing in bonds, shares, currencies, or commodities.

2.**Gather Relevant Data**: To ensure that your analysis is accurate, you should arm yourself with a wide variety of data sources. There is a wealth of information available in the form of economic databases, financial news sites, regulatory filings, and industry reports. Obtain qualitative insights from industry studies and expert comments, in addition to quantitative data such as financial ratios and economic indicators, and use both types of information to your advantage.

The third step is to conduct extensive research. In order to discover ideas that can be put into action, you should delve deeply into the complexities of economic indicators, company financials, and geopolitical events. Establish a methodical strategy for analysing economic indicators, including the evaluation of trends, departures from consensus projections, and the potential impact these variations could have on the market. In a similar manner, investigate the financial affairs of the organisation with a close eye for detail, analysing the most important performance measures, and identifying the underlying trends and abnormalities.

4. **Stay Abreast of Geopolitical Developments**: Keep a close eye on the geopolitical happenings that are influencing the markets around the world. Maintain a close eye on the headlines of the news, geopolitical risk indexes, and expert studies in order to anticipate potential disturbances in the market and evaluate the sentiment of investors. Develop a deep grasp of the geopolitical dynamics that are driving market movements, and adjust your trading techniques in accordance with this understanding.

Incorporate both fundamental and technical analysis into your analysis: You can improve the quality of your trading decisions by combining the insights gained from fundamental analysis with those gained from technical indicators. The combination of fundamental trends with technical indications brings about an increase in the precision of entry and exit points, which in turn enables you to make the most of opportunities for trading that have a high possibility of success.

6. **Conduct an analysis of the risk factors**: Conduct an analysis of the inherent risks that are linked with your trading positions. These risks include economic, financial, and geopolitical hazards. In order to protect your cash and reduce the danger of a loss, you should implement risk management strategies such as stop-loss orders, position sizing, and portfolio diversification.

You should adopt a growth mindset and make a commitment to ongoing learning and adaptation. This is the seventh and last point. Because of the dynamic and ever-changing nature of the financial markets, your trading strategy must be flexible and adaptable in order to be successful. To improve your analytical abilities and keep one step ahead of the competition, it is important to remain aware of developing tendencies, technical breakthroughs, and the ever-changing dynamics of the market.

Through the development of your fundamental analysis abilities and the incorporation of those skills into a disciplined trading technique, you will be able to traverse the complexities of the financial markets with self-assurance and accuracy. It is important to keep in mind that achieving mastery in fundamental analysis is a road that is long and winding, distinguished by perseverance, curiosity, and an unrelenting pursuit of greatness. You should equip yourself with the necessary tools, information, and mindset as you embark on this path. This will allow you to unleash the full potential of fundamental analysis in terms of reaching your trading goals.

Chapter 5: Risk Management Strategies

Trading endeavours that are more likely to be successful are those that have effective risk management. In this chapter, we will discuss a variety of risk management tactics that are necessary for the protection of money and the promotion of long-term profitability in the dynamic world of trading.

Position Sizing:

For the purpose of risk management, position sizing is considered to be one of the key foundations. The process entails making a prudent decision regarding the amount of cash to allocate to each trade, taking into consideration a variety of elements like the level of risk tolerance and the overall size of the account. Traders are able to lessen the impact that prospective losses could have on their portfolios if they adhere to conservative position sizing techniques. The implementation of this strategy guarantees that no single trade will have an undue influence, hence protecting against the occurrence of catastrophic results.

Stop-Loss Orders:

There is a tremendous amount of power that stop-loss orders possess inside the armoury of risk management instruments. In the event that the price hits a certain level, these orders will function as automated instructions to quit a trade. Traders are able to avoid possible losses from occurring by correctly implementing stop-loss orders, which allows them to save capital and prevents minor setbacks from snowballing into big liabilities. Traders are given the ability to retain discipline and adhere to preset risk levels when they embrace stop-loss orders. This is especially beneficial in the context of the natural volatility of financial markets.

Diversification:

A good example of the notion of diversification is the proverb "don't put all your eggs in one basket." Diversification is a strategy that advises spreading risk across a variety of assets or transactions rather than concentrating capital in a single asset or trade. This strategic approach has the purpose of reducing the degree to which bad occurrences have an effect on the portfolio as a whole. Through the adoption of diversity, traders strengthen their defences against unanticipated swings in the market and raise the durability of their investing endeavours.

Hedging:

Hedging is a sophisticated risk management approach that aims to reduce the likelihood of incurring losses at some point in the future. This strategy includes taking stakes in correlated assets that are contradictory to one another in order to counterbalance the underlying risks. Through the systematic implementation of hedging methods, traders are able to protect their portfolios against unfavourable market fluctuations, so promoting stability and reducing the risk of experiencing a loss. The practice of hedging is a strategic instrument that can be utilised to navigate volatile market conditions while simultaneously preserving capital and optimising risk-adjusted returns.

Correlation Analysis:

The use of correlation analysis has emerged as a powerful instrument for identifying the interrelationships that exist between various assets. Traders might discover chances for diversification and risk mitigation by researching correlations through the process of correlation analysis. It is possible for traders to create strong portfolios that are resistant to systemic risks if they have a thorough understanding of the degree of correlation that exists across assets. The utilisation of correlation analysis provides traders with the ability to make well-informed decisions, allowing them to capitalise on the benefits of diversification while simultaneously navigating the complex dynamics of interrelated financial markets.

Conclusion:

To summarise, efficient risk management is the cornerstone of environmentally responsible business practices in the trade industry. A multidimensional approach that includes position sizing, stop-loss orders, diversification, hedging, and correlation analysis is something that traders can use in order to strengthen their defences against market risks and protect their cash. These risk management tactics not only reduce the likelihood of incurring losses, but they also improve the chances of achieving success in trading endeavours over the long term. The wise management of risk acts as a guiding beacon for traders as they negotiate the complexity of the financial markets. It sheds light on the pathways that lead to resilience, success, and the accomplishment of financial goals.

Within the constantly shifting environment of trading, the significance of risk management is something that simply cannot be emphasised. It is not only a tactical factor; rather, it is a strategic need that serves as the basis for the cornerstone of trading prowess. Traders are able to cross turbulent waters with confidence and be in a position to capture chances and triumph over hurdles on their way to achieving financial success if they adhere to effective risk management techniques.

Chapter 6: Establishing Your Trading Routine

When it comes to trading, consistency is fundamental to achieving success. What differentiates profitable traders from the rest of the pack is the consistent and disciplined approach they use. The purpose of this chapter is to look into the essential elements that go into the creation of a healthy trading routine, as well as the ways in which adhering to it may take your trading game to new heights.

Setting Clear Goals and Objectives

With a specific goal in mind, every successful trader starts their trip with a destination in mind. You may establish a road map for your trading endeavours by setting goals that are both clear and attainable. Whether you want to achieve a particular return on investment, become an expert in a particular trading method, or make the shift to trading full-time, identifying your objectives will infuse your trading routine with a sense of purpose and direction.

Distributing Dedicated Trading Resources Time trading is not a hobby; rather, it is a career that requires dedication and concentration on the part of the trader. For the purpose of cultivating discipline and consistency, setting aside certain time intervals for trading activity is essential. By treating trading with the same respect as a regular job, whether it be carving out hours in the morning, afternoon, or both, you can instill a sense of structure in your routine. This will ensure that essential tasks such as market analysis, trade execution, and performance review are prioritised and carried out with diligence.

Continuous Research and Education

It is true that knowledge is power in the ever-changing environment of the financial markets. Putting aside time for learning and research is analogous to honing your weapon in preparation for a fight. The ability to effectively manage market shifts requires that you remain current on market events, economic indicators, and evolving trading tactics. This will equip you with the knowledge necessary to do so. It is non-negotiable for traders who want to prosper in competitive markets to make a commitment to lifelong learning. This commitment can take the form of consuming financial news, digesting market analysis reports, or enrolling in online trading courses.

Through the Implementation of Strong Risk Management Practices
In trading, the protection of capital is of the utmost importance. Maintaining a smart approach to risk management should be in the forefront of your mind before you execute any trade decision. The evaluation of risk-reward ratios, the establishment of stop-loss orders, and the determination of position sizes that are proportional to your risk tolerance and the size of your account are all crucial activities. Through the incorporation of risk management principles into your daily routine, you may protect your capital from receiving an excessive amount of exposure to market volatility, so protecting yourself from suffering catastrophic losses and nurturing longevity in your trading journey.

Regular Performance Evaluation

Self-reflection is the foundation upon which growth is built. You can gain valuable insights into your trading performance by regularly evaluating it. This will assist you to identify your strengths, flaws, and areas in which you can improve. Keeping thorough records of your transactions, analysing both your wins and losses, and finding trends in your decision-making process will provide you the ability to modify your trading approach in an iterative manner. You are able to adjust to shifting market conditions and fine-tune your strategy in order to achieve sustained success over the long term if you adopt a culture of continuous improvement.

The process of developing a systematic trading routine is not limited to simply checking off items on a checklist; rather, it involves incorporating a mindset that is characterised by self-control, resiliency, and continuous education into your trading journey. You may provide the framework for consistent, disciplined trading that will increase your chances of attaining your financial goals by establishing defined goals, assigning dedicated time for trading and education, incorporating solid risk management methods, and performing frequent performance evaluations. These are all things that you can do. Remember that achieving success in trading is not a race; rather, it is a marathon, and a routine that has been carefully crafted serves as your compass, directing you towards your desired goal.

The Acceptance of Adaptability

Flexibility is a trait inherent in successful traders. Although routines are useful for providing structure, they should also leave flexibility for adaptation to the ever-changing conditions of the market. Volatility and unpredictability are prominent characteristics of the financial markets, which are dynamic in nature. In light of this, your trading routine must to be flexible, able to accommodate changes in the dynamics of the market, emerging trends, and events that were not anticipated. Your capacity to quickly pivot and alter your strategies and tactics in order to make the most of opportunities or effectively reduce risks is facilitated by your willingness to embrace adaptability.

Cultivating Mental and Emotional Well-being

In addition to being a game of numbers, trading is also a game at the psychological level. For long-term success, it is essential to possess the skills necessary to keep one's cool in the face of challenges, to effectively handle stress, and to exercise emotional control. It is of the utmost importance to incorporate into your daily routine activities that are beneficial to your mental and emotional well-being. Developing a resilient attitude enables you to handle the ups and downs of the trading experience with equanimity. This can be accomplished by activities such as mindfulness exercises, regular physical activity, or seeking help from other traders or mentors.

Building a Support Network

Although trading is often a solo activity, it does not necessarily have to be a lonely endeavour. The development of a support network consisting of traders who have similar values, mentors, and accountability partners can be quite beneficial. A source of companionship, drive, and perspective can be gained by surrounding oneself with people who are familiar with the difficulties and achievements that are associated with trading. Participating in trading communities, going to networking events, or joining study groups are all examples of ways in which the support of peers may help you feel more confident, speed up your learning, and give a safety net when you are going through difficult times.

Keeping a firm equilibrium

When one is focused on achieving success in trading, it is simple to become engrossed in the markets to the point where one neglects other elements of life. However, in order to ensure long-term sustainability, it is necessary to strike a balance between one's personal well-being and one's trade activities. Your overall well-being can be improved by including into your daily routine time for activities such as relaxing, engaging in hobbies, and spending quality time with loved ones. Keep in mind that trading is not the end in and of itself; rather, it is a means to an end. Through the cultivation of connections, the pursuit of passions outside of trading, and the prioritisation of self-care, you may build a sense of fulfilment that improves both your personal and professional life.

Optimisation Through Iterative Processes

It is not possible to set a trading routine in stone; rather, it is a live, breathing creature that develops over the course of time. Maintain a consistent evaluation and improvement process for your routine, taking into account feedback, experience, and shifting conditions. When trying to determine what works best for you, it is important to experiment with a variety of techniques, timelines, and approaches. Failures should be viewed as chances for growth, and iteration should

be accepted as a means to achieve excellence. Your ability to persevere in the face of adversity and achieve long-term success is directly correlated to your adoption of a mindset that emphasises continuous progress.

As a conclusion, a trading routine that has been carefully developed serves as the basis around which successful trading experiences are constructed. You may establish a framework for sustained success and prosperity in the ever-changing landscape of financial markets by including elements such as adaptability, mental and emotional well-being, a supporting network, balance, and iterative optimisation. This will allow you to take advantage of the opportunities that financial markets present. It is important to keep in mind that not only is trading about making money, but it is also about personal development, resiliency, and the pursuit of mastery. Take pleasure in the process, maintain your self-control, and allow your trading routine to drive you forward towards achieving your objectives.

Chapter 7: Psychology of Trading

A maze of emotions, biases, and mental processes that have a substantial impact on the judgements that traders make and, ultimately, their level of success in the markets is what we mean when we talk about the psychology of trading. We dig into the complex web of psychological elements that drive trading behaviour in this chapter, and we investigate various tactics that can be utilised to cultivate the mental discipline that is essential for successfully navigating the hurdles that are commonly encountered in the trading industry.

Emotional Rollercoaster: Fear and Greed

In the minds of traders, fear and greed are two formidable foes that are ready to wreck even the most well-thought-out tactics. Fear and greed are two of the most powerful adversaries. It is possible for traders to get paralysed by the fear of losing money, which can cause them to pause or detour from their trading strategies out of an unreasonable drive to prevent prospective losses at all costs. Traders can be blinded by greed, which can cause them to take unnecessary risks or cling to lost positions in the expectation of a miracle turnaround. On the other hand, greed can blind traders.

It is necessary for traders to first recognise and recognise the presence of these emotional traps before they can avoid them. Traders are able to take a step back and reevaluate the issue with a clear head if they are able to recognise when fear or greed begins to influence their decision-making process. It is possible to lessen the impact of fear and greed by putting risk management tactics into action. These strategies include setting stop-loss orders and determining the size of positions. This enables traders to make decisions that are more sensible and disciplined.

The Overconfidence Trap

When it comes to the realm of trading, getting successful can be a double-edged sword, as it frequently results in overconfidence and complacency. When traders make a string of winning deals, they may begin to assume that they have mastered the markets. This might cause them to take risks that are not necessary or to overlook the protocols that are important for risk management strategies. On the other hand, the fact of the matter is that the markets are intrinsically unpredictable, and no amount of success in the past can ensure the achievement of future results.

A good dosage of humility and scepticism is something that traders need to keep in their arsenal in order to avoid slipping into the trap of overconfidence. Traders should try to avoid concentrating on their previous achievements and instead concentrate on continuously improving their skills and adapting to the ever-changing conditions of the market. It is possible for traders to avoid making mistakes that are financially detrimental and to maintain long-term success in the markets if they have a humble attitude and acknowledge that there is always more to learn.

The Virtue of Patience

Patience is frequently eclipsed by the attraction of immediate profits and instant gratification in the world of trading, which is characterised by a fast-paced environment. Having patience, on the other hand, is a virtue that can have a huge impact on the performance of a trader. Because of the irregular and unpredictable nature of the market, it is not unusual for traders to face periods of setback or stagnation in their trading activity. At a time when things are difficult, patience is more important than ever since it enables traders to maintain their concentration on their long-term objectives and to resist the temptation to pursue gains in the short term.

The cultivation of patience calls for self-control and a determination to persevere through periods of momentary failure. The ability to trust one's trading plans and to resist the desire to depart from those plans at the first hint of difficulty is a skill that traders need to acquire. When traders are able to preserve patience and remain steadfast in their methods, they are able to manoeuvre through turbulent market conditions with confidence and resilience.

The Discipline Imperative

When it comes to the psychological characteristics that are necessary for effective trading, discipline is the most important. Even the most meticulously constructed trading plan is doomed to fail if it is not accompanied with discipline. The ability to constantly adhere to a set of rules and principles, regardless of the influence of external variables or emotional impulses, is what we mean when we talk about discipline.

Self-awareness, self-control, and resiliency are elements that must be present in order to successfully maintain discipline. Traders need to develop a mindset that allows them to remain unwaveringly committed to their trading goals, even when they are confronted with challenges. To accomplish this, it is necessary to adhere to the risk management rules that have been defined, to rigorously monitor trading indications, and to avoid making rash judgements that are motivated by emotions.

**

Cultivating Mental Discipline**

The process of cultivating the mental discipline that is necessary for successful trading is an ongoing one that calls for full commitment and consistent practice. The discipline of traders can be strengthened via the use of a variety of approaches, including journaling, visualisation exercises, and mindfulness meditation.

Trading professionals can benefit from practicing mindfulness meditation because it enables them to remain present and focused, allowing them to monitor their thoughts and feelings without being carried away by them. Participants in trading exercises can mentally rehearse their trading methods and reinforce favourable habits through the use of visualisation exercises. Journaling gives traders the opportunity to reflect on their transactions, pinpoint areas in which they could improve, and hold themselves accountable for the activities they take.

Conclusion

When it comes to achieving success in the markets, having a solid understanding of the psychology behind trading is absolutely necessary. In order to improve their odds of attaining their financial goals and successfully navigating the complexity of the trading world, traders can improve their chances of recognising and regulating their emotions, retaining humility and patience, and fostering steadfast discipline. Always keep in mind that trading is just as much a mental game as it is a technical one, and that understanding the psychological aspects is absolutely necessary for long-term growth and success.

Chapter 8: Advanced Trading Strategies

The attractiveness of advanced trading strategies becomes increasingly appealing as traders improve their abilities and gain expertise in navigating the complex waters of the financial markets. This is because advanced trading methods are more complex than traditional trading strategies. The implementation of these techniques, which are typically reserved for seasoned professionals, has the potential to increase profitability and provides the opportunity to capitalise on the nuances of market dynamics. The following four advanced trading strategies are discussed in this chapter: trend following, mean reversion, pairs trading, and arbitrage.

Trend Following: A Pillar of Market Momentum

One of the most important strategies that experienced traders have at their disposal is known as trend following. In its most fundamental form, trend following is centred on the process of recognising and capitalising on established market trends. The objective of traders who utilise this technique is to capitalise on the momentum of the market by entering positions that are in line with the dominant trend and quickly leaving positions before any indications of a reversal appear. A good trend following strategy requires patience, discipline, and a keen eye for distinguishing actual trends from noise, despite the fact that it appears to be a basic methodology. Traders have the ability to harness the force of market momentum to increase their profits if they adhere to stringent risk management measures and exercise patience.

Mean Reversion: Profiting from Market Oscillations

Mean reversion, on the other hand, is based on taking advantage of market fluctuations and gradually returning prices to their long-term averages. This is in contrast to trend following. Market participants who use the mean reversion strategy look for overbought or oversold levels in order to anticipate a return to the mean. This method is most successful in range-bound markets, which are characterised by cycles of expansion and contraction that alternate with one another. The execution of mean reversion trades, on the other hand, requires precision timing and sophisticated risk management in order to reduce losses over extended trends. Through the utilisation of robust statistical analysis and the development of their timing instincts, traders are able to capitalise on the profit potential that is inherent in market oscillations.

Pairs Trading: Harnessing Correlation for Profit

By taking advantage of momentary price differences between two correlated assets, pairs trading is able to capitalise on the relationship that exists between these assets. In order to take advantage of price differences, traders look for pairings of assets that have a certain historical connection and then execute simultaneous long and short positions on those assets. One of the most fundamental aspects of pairs trading is the anticipation that the prices of assets that are connected will eventually begin to converge. The execution of this approach necessitates not only a profound comprehension of the fundamental connection that exists between the assets, but also a vigilant monitoring of the market conditions in order to grab chances that are ephemeral. Pairs traders have the ability to unlock possible profit opportunities in volatile market settings if they are able to demonstrate a mastery of the complexities of correlation and divergence.

Arbitrage: Capturing Risk-Free Profit Opportunities

The highest level of trading sophistication is represented by arbitrage, which offers the possibility of making money without taking any risks by taking advantage of price differences between different markets. Individuals who engage in arbitrage take advantage of inefficiencies in pricing by simultaneously purchasing assets that are undervalued in one market and selling them at a higher price in another market. Although arbitrage chances are transitory and require a technological infrastructure that is technologically advanced in order to capitalise on them, they have the potential to deliver big rewards for traders who are perceptive. When pursuing arbitrage, it is necessary to maintain unrelenting vigilance, execute with lightning speed, and have a comprehensive understanding of the microstructure of several markets. By being proficient in the art of arbitrage, traders have the ability to open up a world of unrivalled profit potential in the context of the global financial landscape.

Conclusion: Navigating the Advanced Terrain

For experienced traders who are looking to improve their performance and increase their profits, advanced trading methods are a guiding light that can help them achieve their goals. Whether it is by riding the waves of market momentum through trend following, profiting from oscillations with mean reversion, leveraging correlation in pairs trading, or capturing risk-free returns via arbitrage, traders have the ability to broaden their toolkit and adapt to a variety of market situations. On the other hand, in order to successfully implement these tactics, one must possess a combination of technical expertise, self-control, and organisational skills. Traders may navigate the ever-changing terrain of the financial markets with confidence and precision if they have mastered the complexities of advanced trading methods. This places them in a position to achieve consistent success in their pursuit of profit.

Chapter 9: Day Trading vs. Swing Trading

Within the ever-changing realm of the financial markets, traders are confronted with a plethora of trading techniques from which to select, each of which presents its own distinct collection of chances and obstacles. The day trading and swing trading strategies stand out as two of the most prominent ways among them. It is possible for traders to better match their strategies with their objectives, risk tolerance, and personal preferences if they have a thorough understanding of the unique characteristics of each.

Taking advantage of short-term price swings that occur during the period of a single trading day is the objective of day trading, which is comparable to the sprinter compared to other types of trading. To be successful in this endeavour, one must possess a high level of concentration, self-control, and the capacity to make snap judgements in the face of very volatile markets. Individuals who engage in day trading frequently make use of technical analysis and intraday charts in order to spot patterns and trends. They then execute many trades throughout the day in order to capitalise on minor price differences. Due to the rapid speed, traders are required to maintain a state of alertness and agility.

On the other hand, swing trading takes a more methodical approach, which is analogous to how a marathon runner paces himself for the duration of the race. Traders are able to capitalise on medium-term trends within the context of bigger market cycles by employing this approach, which entails holding positions over a period of time ranging from several days to weeks. In order to identify probable entry and exit opportunities, swing traders employ a combination of fundamental and technical analysis. Their objective is to ride the momentum of a trend for as long as feasible. When compared to day trading, this strategy provides traders with more freedom and less stress because they have more time to analyse market movements and make decisions based on that analysis.

As far as day trading and swing trading are concerned, the fundamental difference resides in the timeframe in which deals are executed. Traders that engage in day trading thrive on the volatility of intraday price swings, which allows them to enter and exit positions within minutes or hours. Swing traders, on the other hand, are able to maintain their positions for longer periods of time, which enables them to endure volatility in the short term and capitalise on bigger market trends. The methods, tools, and mentality that are necessary for success in each approach are determined by the discrepancy in timeframes that exist between them.

The amount of capital that is required for each plan is another essential aspect to take into consideration. As a result of the high frequency of trades and the obligation to meet minimum account balance criteria established by brokers, day trading typically requires bigger sums of capital than other types of trading in general. Swing trading, on the other hand, can be carried out with a lesser amount of money because positions are held for longer periods of time. This reduces the requirement for frequent trading activity and so mitigates the expenses associated with transactions.

Although day trading and swing trading include different concerns, risk management is of the utmost importance in both types of trading. Day traders have to handle the inherent volatility of intraday markets, which requires them to use tight stop-loss orders and execute trades quickly in order to reduce the amount of possible losses they could incur. On the other hand, swing traders are required to deal with overnight risks, which include market gaps and unexpected news events that have the potential to influence positions that have been held for longer periods of time. For the purpose of maintaining capital and protecting against unfavourable market conditions, it is vital to implement risk management methods that are carefully considered and executed, such as position sizing and diversification.

In the end, the decision between day trading and swing trading is determined by the preferences of the individual, their level of risk tolerance, and their trading objectives. In spite of the fact that day trading is characterised by the appeal of quick profits and action-packed excitement, it requires unwavering concentration and discipline in the face of turbulent market conditions. Traders are able to capitalise on broader market trends while keeping a healthy work-life balance when they engage in swing trading, which offers a more relaxed pace than traditional traditional trading.

It is important for traders to undertake extensive study, backtesting, and self-evaluation before beginning any technique. This will allow them to determine which approach is most suitable for their personality and goals. There is the possibility for profitability and success in the markets through both day trading and swing trading; however, the ability of the trader to adapt, evolve, and execute their chosen strategy with accuracy and discipline is ultimately the most important factor in determining whether or not they will be successful.

To summarise, regardless of whether you are drawn to the fast-paced approach of day trading or the measured approach of swing trading, the key to success is in knowing the complexities of each trading technique and aligning them with your individual trading style and goals. You will be able to navigate the complexities of the financial markets with confidence and accomplish your trading goals if you carefully consider the benefits and drawbacks of each strategy and hone your skills through practice and experience.

Chapter 10: Options and Futures Trading

Options and futures trading are examples of complex instruments that are used in the financial markets. These techniques provide traders with the opportunity to make big gains and the capacity to properly control risk. We will delve into the foundations of options and futures trading in this chapter. We will get a knowledge of the mechanics that underlie these markets, and we will investigate the many methods that traders utilise in order to capitalise on market changes.

Understanding Options Trading

Options are derivative contracts that give the holder the right, but not the responsibility, to purchase or sell an underlying asset at a predefined price (the striking price) within a certain timeframe (until the expiration date). However, the holder is not required to exercise this right. The holder of a call option is granted the right to purchase the underlying asset, whereas the holder of a put option is granted the obligation to sell the asset. When it comes to options trading, one of the most significant benefits is the ability to leverage positions while simultaneously limiting the risk of loss to the premium that is paid for the option.

Exploring Futures Trading

Futures contracts, on the other hand, bind the buyer to acquire (or the seller to sell) the underlying asset at a predefined price on a future date that has been established. The great liquidity and transparency of these contracts are ensured by the fact that they are standardised and traded on an organised exchange. Speculators are able to place wagers on the prospective price fluctuations of a wide range of assets through the use of futures trading. These assets include commodities such as oil and gold, as well as financial instruments such as stock indices and currencies. Additionally, futures contracts are considered to be essential hedging tools for firms and investors who are looking to reduce the risk of severe price swings.

Common Strategies in Options and Futures Trading

1. Directional Strategies

When a trader believes that the underlying asset will see bullish price fluctuations, they will use the approach known as "buying call options." When traders buy call options, they have the opportunity to profit from price appreciation while restricting their possible losses to the amount of the premium that they have paid. Put options are used by traders to profit from unfavourable price changes. On the other hand, put options are purchased by other traders. Through the purchase of put options, traders are able to capitalise on falling prices while also limiting their exposure to potential losses.

2. Income Generation Strategies - *Selling Covered Call Options*: Traders with a long stock position can generate additional income by selling call options against their holdings. One method of trading, which is referred to as a covered call, involves selling call options while simultaneously retaining an equivalent amount of shares in order to cover the possible liability. By selling put options, traders have the opportunity to possibly acquire the underlying asset at a discount. This is referred to as "selling cash-secured put options." Keeping cash on hand that is equivalent to the strike price multiplied by the number of contracts sold is required for this method. This cash is used as collateral to meet any potential obligations that may arise.

3. **Advanced Strategies** - *Options Spreads*: These strategies involve simultaneously buying and selling multiple options contracts to limit risk and potentially enhance returns. Vertical spreads, such as bull spreads and bear spreads, are two examples. Complex methods, such as iron condors, which incorporate several legs and strike prices, are another example.

4. Futures Trading Strategies

This type of trading is known as "speculative trading," and it involves traders taking long or short positions in futures contracts in order to bet on the future price movements of commodities, currencies, or financial instruments. When investors want to protect themselves from unfavourable price swings in the underlying asset, they utilise futures contracts as a form of hedging. As an illustration, a farmer might protect themselves from the possibility of crop prices falling by selling futures contracts in order to get a favourable price.

Risk Management Considerations

Trading in options and futures carries with it a number of inherent dangers, one of which is the possibility of suffering significant losses. In order to be successful in trading, it is essential for traders to have a solid understanding of the dangers that are connected with leverage, the volatility of the market, and the many trading methods. When it comes to efficiently controlling downside risk and protecting money, risk management tactics such as position sizing, setting stop-loss orders, and diversification are absolutely necessary.

Conclusion

Options and futures trading provide traders with a wide variety of chances to profit from price fluctuations in a variety of asset classes while effectively controlling risk. Such opportunities are available to traders. Within the ever-changing realm of the financial markets, traders have the ability to diversify their portfolios, protect themselves from the hazards associated with the market, and perhaps increase their overall profits if they have mastered the mechanics of options and futures contracts and implemented effective trading techniques. Nevertheless, in order for traders to successfully manage the complexities of options and futures trading, it is vital that they approach these products with prudence, completing extensive research, and maintaining discipline in their trading approach.

Chapter 11: Strategies for Successful Cryptocurrency Trading

The trading of cryptocurrencies has brought about a change in the financial landscape, providing investors with chances that have never been seen before to capitalise on the turbulent yet exciting digital asset market. This chapter will look into the techniques and principles that can guide traders towards success in navigating the complexity of bitcoin trading. These strategies and principles can be found in this chapter.

1. Understanding Market Dynamics:

The markets for cryptocurrencies are open around the clock, including weekends and holidays, giving traders the ability to engage in trading activity whenever they choose. However, because of this ongoing availability, there is also the possibility that price fluctuations will occur quickly and without warning. Traders are need to maintain vigilance and conduct regular market monitoring in order to properly manage risks and capitalise on opportunities that could result in positive outcomes.

2. Embracing Volatility:

The trading of cryptocurrencies is characterised by a high degree of volatility, as values are subject to rapid swings within relatively short timescales. Despite the fact that volatility can be a source of risk, it also offers the possibility of making big rewards. In order to reduce the likelihood of incurring losses, traders should be willing to accept volatility and employ robust risk management measures. These strategies include the establishment of stop-loss orders and the diversification of their portfolios.

3. Assessing Liquidity:

In bitcoin trading, liquidity is an essential component that plays a role in determining the transaction fees and the ease with which deals may be executed. It is recommended that traders give high priority to highly liquid cryptocurrencies such as Bitcoin and Ethereum since these cryptocurrencies offer tighter spreads and deeper order books. Additionally, users should exercise caution while trading alternative cryptocurrencies that have a lower liquidity, and they should undertake extensive research in order to mitigate the dangers that are linked with lesser liquidity.

4. Utilizing Technical Analysis:

The use of technical analysis is essential in the trading of cryptocurrencies since it enables traders to make educated judgements by utilising past price data and market patterns as their primary sources of information. Through the utilisation of chart patterns, indicators, and various other technical tools, traders are able to identify prospective entry and exit positions, as well as anticipate trend reversals with a higher degree of precision.

5. Staying Informed:

It is possible for regulatory developments and security concerns to have a substantial impact on the cryptocurrency market, which can in turn influence pricing and the emotions of investors. Traders are required to do exhaustive due diligence prior to engaging in any trades, as well as to remain informed about changes in regulatory requirements and any security threats. Traders are able to adjust their strategies appropriately and reduce the likelihood of potential dangers if they remain current on essential news and events from the market.

6. Employing Risk Management Strategies:

It is absolutely necessary to have efficient risk management in order to achieve long-term success in bitcoin trading. In order to develop clear risk tolerance levels and adhere to tight money management rules, traders should restrict the size of their positions and diversify their portfolios. Traders should also establish clear risk tolerance levels. In addition, the utilisation of hedging measures and the prudent utilisation of leverage can be of assistance in mitigating potential losses and managing capital preservation.

7. Continuous Learning and Adaptation:

As a result of the dynamic and ever-changing nature of the cryptocurrency market, traders are required to be resilient in the face of shifting market conditions and developing trends. Participating in trade communities, attending educational seminars, or engaging in self-study are all excellent ways to continue your education and ensure that you remain one step ahead of the competition. It is possible for traders to increase their overall performance and refine their tactics if they maintain their flexibility and remain open to developing new ideas.

8. Psychological Discipline:

When it comes to trading cryptocurrencies, emotions have the potential to obscure judgement and create impulsive decision-making. Individuals who engage in trading are required to establish psychological discipline and keep a sensible perspective, especially when confronted with market swings and problems that are not anticipated. When it comes to trading, the ability to exercise patience, resilience, and emotional control can assist traders in making rational judgements that are founded on logic and analysis rather than fear or greed.

To summarise, in order to be successful in trading cryptocurrencies, one must possess a combination of strategic planning, technical expertise, risk management, and psychological discipline. Traders may confidently navigate this fascinating and rewarding market if they have a solid understanding of the specific dynamics of the cryptocurrency market and if they execute trading techniques that are strong. Nevertheless, it is of the utmost importance to approach trading in cryptocurrencies with prudence and diligence, recognising the inherent risks while also grabbing opportunities for profit and growth.

Chapter 12: Building a Diverse Portfolio

When it comes to smart investing, diversification is the cornerstone since it provides a defence mechanism against the unpredictability that is inevitably present in the financial markets. The purpose of this chapter is to delve into the complexities of building a well-rounded portfolio, as well as to investigate the numerous advantages that such a portfolio offers and the methods that can be utilised to attain it.

At its most fundamental level, diversification refers to the process of distributing one's investing money across a wide range of asset classes, geographical locations, and industries. Investors strive to minimise risk while simultaneously optimising profits by acting in this manner. This approach is analogous to the idea of not putting all of your eggs in one basket; in the case that unfavourable occurrences have an effect on a particular asset or market, the impact on the whole portfolio is mitigated by the behaviour of other assets.

The decrease of risk is one of the most significant benefits that diversification contributes. It is possible for investors to lessen the impact of market downturns or volatility in any one asset class by spreading their investments over a variety of assets that have low correlations with one another. For instance, during times of volatility in the stock market, assets such as bonds or commodities may provide stability, which can assist in the preservation of capital and the maintenance of portfolio resilience.

In addition, diversification improves risk-adjusted returns by achieving a balance between the likelihood of loss and the potential for gain. The ability to produce a more constant level of performance over time is something that investors can accomplish by combining assets that have diverse risk profiles.

When navigating tumultuous market situations, this stability is especially beneficial because a varied portfolio can help weather storms and sustain wealth amid uncertain economic landscapes. For this reason, a diversified portfolio is particularly valuable.

Besides reducing the likelihood of adverse outcomes, diversification enables investors to get access to a wider range of investment alternatives. Under different market conditions, many asset classes display a variety of performance characteristics that are distinct from one another. Investors are able to capitalise on a wide variety of market trends and possibilities for profit by diversifying their holdings across a variety of asset classes, including stocks, bonds, real estate, and alternative assets. This allows them to protect themselves from the peculiarities of any one market segment.

It is necessary to give careful consideration to asset allocation, which is the strategic distribution of investments across a variety of asset classes, in order to construct a portfolio that is varied. The risk tolerance, financial goals, and time horizon of the investors should all be taken into consideration when allocating this allocation. The judgements on asset allocation are further informed by factors such as age, income, investment experience, and market forecast. This allows the portfolio to be tailored to the specific circumstances of each individual.

The process of asset allocation can be carried out through a wide variety of investment vehicles, including conventional mutual funds and exchange-traded funds (ETFs), as well as individual securities and alternative investments. Every investment vehicle comes with its own set of benefits and dangers, tailoring itself to the interests and goals of a wide range of investors. Furthermore, diversification strategies such as frequent rebalancing ensure that the portfolio continues to maintain the risk-return profile that the investor desires over the course of time, thereby adjusting to the ever-changing market conditions and the requirements of the investor.

To put it simply, constructing a diversified portfolio is of the utmost importance for achieving long-term financial success and durability. Investors can improve their risk-adjusted returns, capture varied market opportunities, and pursue their financial goals with confidence if they spread their assets over a variety of asset classes, sectors, and regions. Investors are given the ability to negotiate uncertainties and seek wealth accumulation with prudence and insight when they take advantage of diversification, which acts as a bulwark against the variations that occur in the financial markets.

As a conclusion, diversification is not only a wise investing technique; rather, it is an essential component of a financially secure financial situation. By embracing diversification, investors are able to protect their portfolios from the volatility of the market, maximise their risk-adjusted returns, and open up a world of options for investment. Investors are able to chart a course towards long-term prosperity by using a broad portfolio as their compass. This course of action is strengthened by the resilience and adaptability that are inherent in a well-balanced investment plan.

Chapter 13: Trading in Volatile Markets

Volatility is a property that is characteristic of financial markets, and trading in situations that are turbulent demands a specific set of abilities and methods. In this chapter, we will discuss the strategies that traders can use to successfully traverse tumultuous markets, efficiently capitalise on opportunities, and effectively manage risk.

Managing one's emotions is one of the most significant obstacles that comes with investing in unpredictable markets. Volatility can cause traders to experience increased feelings of fear and uncertainty, which can lead to traders making rash judgements or abandoning their trading plans entirely. Despite fluctuations in the market, it is necessary for traders to maintain their composure and discipline in the face of unpredictable conditions. They must also adhere to their trading strategy and the regulations that govern risk management.

Because price swings can be sudden and unpredictable, risk management is especially important in markets that are currently experiencing volatility. For the purpose of safeguarding their capital and minimising losses during times of increased volatility, traders should implement strategies like as position sizing, stop-loss orders, and diversification. When taking into consideration the increased market risk, it is also vital to modify the size of positions and the amount of risk exposure.

When trading in volatile markets, one of the most important aspects to consider is how to adjust to shifting market conditions. As a result of the fact that volatility can present traders with both opportunities and challenges, it is necessary for them to adopt an approach that is both flexible and open-minded. Traders might need to make adjustments to their trading technique, time frame, or risk tolerance in order to adapt shifting market dynamics and capitalise on developing trends.

Because it can assist traders in recognising crucial support and resistance levels, trend patterns, and potential reversal signals, technical analysis can be especially helpful in markets that are characterised by high levels of volatility. Traders are able to make trading decisions that are more informed and manage volatile conditions with greater confidence when they analyse price activity and market characteristics.

In addition to providing useful insights into market trends and potential causes for volatility, fundamental research can also provide valuable insights through the use of technical analysis. It is important for traders to maintain a level of awareness regarding economic data, company earnings reports, and geopolitical events that have the potential to influence investors' attitude and cause price fluctuations.

To add insult to injury, the process of constructing a portfolio that is rich in diversity is not a one-time endeavour but rather a continuing journey. All of these things—market dynamics, economic landscapes, and human circumstances—are always shifting and evolving. As a result, it is vital to conduct frequent reviews and adjustments of the portfolio in order to guarantee that it continues to match with the objectives and levels of risk tolerance of the investors.

Reviewing the portfolio on a regular basis provides the opportunity to evaluate the performance of individual assets, assess the trends in the market, and make any required adjustments to the asset allocation. This preventative strategy gives investors the ability to capitalise on developing opportunities while simultaneously reducing the likelihood of potential hazards. The process of rebalancing the portfolio, which involves modifying the allocation of assets in order to maintain the correct risk levels, is another method that assists in realigning the portfolio with its intended goals.

Incorporating the concepts of diversity into the creation of a portfolio needs careful study and strategic planning. During the process of selecting assets, investors should take into consideration a variety of aspects, including asset class correlations, past performance, and future growth potential. Investors can achieve greater risk reduction and enhance the stability of their portfolios by diversifying their holdings among asset classes that have low correlations when they diversify their portfolios.

In addition, geographic diversification is an essential component in limiting the risks that are linked with geopolitical events, fluctuations in currency, and economic downturns in specific regions. In order to mitigate the effects of localised risks and get exposure to chances for global growth, it is beneficial to invest in assets that are located across a variety of countries and regions. By distributing assets over multiple geographic locations, a portfolio can become more resilient and less susceptible to the effects of any one market or economic climate.

At the same time that they are working towards diversity, investors should keep in mind the fees, taxes, and other costs that are involved with the various investment products. Despite the fact that diversity can be helpful in mitigating risks, high fees can reduce the returns on investments over time. Consequently, the selection of investment vehicles that are efficient in terms of cost and the reduction of expenses that are not necessary are essential components of a successful diversification plan.

In conclusion, one of the most important aspects of smart investment is the construction of a portfolio that is diverse. By diversifying their holdings across a variety of asset classes, industries, and geographical regions, investors can lower their exposure to risk, increase their returns, and take advantage of a wide range of exciting investment opportunities. Investors are able to negotiate the complexity of the financial markets with confidence and resilience, ultimately attaining their long-term financial goals, if they carefully allocate their assets, conduct periodic reviews, and strategically rebalance their portfolios.

Chapter 14: Leveraging Technology in Trading

For traders all around the world, technological improvements have become the most important factor in determining their level of success in the ever-changing world of trading. The technologies that are currently available provide chances that have never been seen before to improve decision-making, optimise tactics, and eventually achieve better profitability in the markets. These techniques include algorithmic trading, artificial intelligence (AI), and machine learning.

Algorithmic Trading: The Power of Automation

The execution of deals in the financial markets has been completely transformed as a result of the introduction of algorithmic trading, which is also frequently referred to as automated or black-box trading. This allows traders to automate the execution of transactions based on pre-defined criteria such as price changes, volume, and market indicators. Traders can do this by harnessing the power of computer algorithms. Traders are able to execute deals with lightning speed and precision because to this automation, which allows them to capitalise on opportunities that are only available for a limited period of time and manage risk more efficiently.

The advantages of using algorithmic trading are numerous and varied. In the first place, it eliminates the emotional biases that are frequently experienced by human traders, making it possible to make decisions solely on the basis of both data and logic. In the second place, it makes it possible to keep an eye on the markets around the clock, which gives traders the ability to take advantage of chances that come up outside of the typical trading hours. The last benefit of algorithmic trading is that it makes it easier to backtest and optimise trading techniques. This gives traders the ability to tweak their approaches and easily adjust to shifting market conditions.

AI and Machine Learning: Predictive Power Unleashed

Traders who are attempting to get a competitive edge in the markets have found that artificial intelligence and machine learning have emerged as useful tools. Traders are able to make judgements that are better educated and execute trades that are more profitable thanks to artificial intelligence and machine learning algorithms. These algorithms analyse large amounts of data, recognise trends, and make predictions about future market movements.

The development of predictive models, the optimisation of trading strategies, and the automation of decision-making processes are only some of the varied applications that can be made use of these technologies. For instance, machine learning algorithms can be taught to recognise intricate patterns in market data. This enables traders to recognise trends and anomalies that may not be obvious to the naked eye of a human being. Additionally, trading systems that are powered by AI are able to continuously learn from previous trading experiences, thereby refining their methods over time in order to react to the ever-changing dynamics of the market.

Advanced Trading Platforms: Streamlining Workflow

An increase in the number of sophisticated trading platforms and software tools has provided traders with more capabilities, including the ability to optimise their trading workflow and have access to real-time market data and analysis. A broad variety of features and functionalities, such as charts that may be customised, technical indicators, and order execution tools, are provided by these platforms. These features and functionalities enable traders to execute trades in a quick and efficient manner.

As an additional point of interest, numerous trading platforms now provide integrated artificial intelligence-driven analytics and trading algorithms. This makes it possible for traders to take advantage of cutting-edge technology without the requirement of extensive programming skills. A level playing field has been created as a result of the democratisation of technology, which has made it possible for traders of all skill levels to gain access to the tools and resources that were previously reserved for institutional investors.

Mobile Trading Apps: Trading on the Go

The introduction of mobile trading applications has brought about a sea change in the manner in which traders maintain their portfolios and carry out trades. Trading apps for mobile devices provide traders who are constantly on the move with an unprecedented level of flexibility and convenience. These apps allow traders to watch markets and place deals from any location and at any time.

It is possible for traders to maintain a connection to the markets and grasp chances as they present themselves thanks to the fact that these mobile applications offer the same features and functionality as their desktop versions. As a result of the strength of mobile technology, traders are now able to stay ahead of the curve and execute deals with ease, regardless of whether they are travelling around the world or commuting to work.

Social Trading Platforms: Learning from the Collective Wisdom

In conclusion, the proliferation of social trading platforms and online communities has made it feasible for traders to learn from one another and interact in ways that were before impossible. This has resulted in the democratisation of access to trading information and insights. In order to enhance their trading performance over time and acquire useful knowledge, traders can increase their trading performance by following and duplicating the trades of successful investors.

Through the use of these platforms, traders are able to debate trading ideas, share insights, and learn from each other's experiences. Additionally, these platforms promote the sharing of knowledge and collaboration among traders. This allows traders to draw into the collective wisdom of the crowd and make more educated judgements in the markets. This can be accomplished through the use of social media channels, chat rooms, and forums.

Conclusion

The trading scene has been completely revolutionised as a result of technological advancements, which have provided traders with access to tools, resources, and opportunities that were previously unavailable. There is a plethora of alternatives available to traders, ranging from algorithmic trading and artificial intelligence to advanced trading platforms, mobile applications, and social trading networks. These options allow traders to improve their decision-making abilities, execute transactions in a more efficient manner, and eventually achieve greater success in the markets. It is possible for traders to position themselves for success in a trading environment that is becoming increasingly competitive and dynamic if they use these technologies and remain ahead of the curve.

Chapter 15: Long-Term Investing Strategies

Introduction:

Long-term investing is a guiding light towards stability and progress in the ever-changing world of finance, where markets are prone to fluctuations and trends come and go. It is the determined approach that has been able to withstand the storms of the economy and has produced considerable returns for investors who have been patient. The purpose of this chapter is to provide a road map for the construction and maintenance of a robust investment portfolio by delving into the fundamental ideas and techniques that underpin effective long-term investing.

The Fundamentals of Long-Term Investing:

An unwavering dedication to basic analysis and an in-depth comprehension of asset value are the two principles that form the foundation of long-term investing. Rather than giving in to the temptation of short-term gains or attempting to time the market, long-term investors adopt a patient mindset and look for assets that are inexpensive yet have the potential to expand significantly. With this strategy, the force of compounding may be utilised to magnify returns over a period of time, so transforming more modest assets into large riches.

Value Investing: A Timeless Strategy:

The value investing philosophy, which was made famous by luminaries such as Benjamin Graham and Warren Buffett, continues to appeal with investors who are looking for returns that are long-lasting. Through the rigorous evaluation of companies based on measures such as earnings, cash flow, and assets, value investors are able to uncover opportunities in which market prices deviate from the underlying worth of the product or service. They intend to reap the benefits of market inefficiencies being corrected by themselves, which will bring prices closer to fair value, by choosing their investments with discipline and holding them for an extended period of time.

Growth Investing: Nurturing Tomorrow's Titans:

In the realm of growth investing, where investors look for businesses that are set for exponential expansion and disruptive transformation, innovation is the energy that drives the process. These forward-thinking investors are ready to pay a premium for businesses that have great growth potential because they are betting on the ability of these businesses to outrun the expectations of the market and offer higher returns over the sustained period of time. Growth investors put themselves in a position to seize the next wave of market leaders by leveraging the power of innovation and remaining alert to the ever-changing trends in the industry.

Dividend Investing: Harvesting Sustainable Income:

Investors that place a high priority on the development of income might benefit from dividend investing since it provides a compelling method for constructing a consistent supply of cash flow. Dividend investors develop portfolios that are designed to deliver steady income year after year by concentrating on firms that have a history of making consistent dividend payments and a commitment to increasing shareholder value. Through the process of reinvesting dividends and taking advantage of the compounding effect, they are able to establish a solid basis for the long-term building of wealth while simultaneously receiving a consistent income from their investments.

Strategic Asset Allocation: Balancing Risk and Reward:

When it comes to long-term investment, diversification is the most important factor in risk management since it enables investors to disperse their wealth across a wide variety of asset classes, industries, and geographical regions. When investors avoid overexposure to any one investment and keep their portfolios well-balanced, they are able to reduce the negative effects of market volatility and maintain their capital during times of turmoil. In addition, doing regular portfolio rebalancing helps to ensure that asset allocations continue to be in line with investing goals, allowing investors to make the most of opportunities while protecting themselves from taking on an excessive amount of risk.

Conclusion:

An uncompromising dedication to the values of patience, discipline, and fundamental analysis is required for long-term investing strategies. Long-term investing is not just a technique; it is a mindset. When it comes to navigating the intricate landscape of the financial markets, investors have a wide variety of instruments at their disposal. These tools include value investing, growth investing, dividend investing, and strategic asset allocation. Investors are able to construct and cultivate a resilient portfolio that can withstand the test of time by keeping committed to their long-term objectives, maintaining a focus on long-term goals, and responding to changing market conditions. This allows investors to secure their financial security for future generations.

Chapter 16: Conclusion

Now that we have reached the last chapter of this book, it is time to take a moment to think on the journey that we have travelled together and the important realisations that we have acquired along the way. We have covered a wide range of topics with the goal of assisting you in becoming a more knowledgeable and effective trader. These topics vary from learning the fundamentals of trading to studying advanced methods and making use of technology. This conclusion will present you with a summary of the most important takeaways, with some concluding comments, and with some direction for your future trading endeavours.

We have emphasised the significance of education and preparation in the trading industry throughout the entirety of this book. Continuous learning is vital for staying informed about market trends, polishing your trading skills, and responding to changing market conditions. This statement holds true regardless of whether you are just starting out or have years of experience in the trading industry. You have taken a significant step towards accomplishing your monetary objectives by devoting your time and energy to the process of acquiring understanding of the foundations of trading.

One of the most important ideas that has been discussed throughout this book is the need of having a reliable trading plan. The purpose of a trading plan is to act as a road map for your trading operations by detailing your objectives, methods, rules for risk management, and criteria for entering and leaving deals. Maintaining discipline, reducing the amount of emotional decision-making, and increasing your chances of success in the markets are all possible outcomes that can be achieved through the development and implementation of a distinct trading plan.

Another important topic that has been brought up in our conversations is risk management. When it comes to trading, risk management is of the utmost importance because losses are an unavoidable part of the journey. Through the utilisation of risk management strategies, such as position sizing, stop-loss orders, and diversification, you are able to safeguard your capital and maintain the integrity of your trading account during times of market turbulence. It is important to keep in mind that the goal is not to completely prevent losses but rather to efficiently manage them in order to secure long-term profitability.

In addition, we have investigated a wide range of trading tactics, ranging from fundamental research and technical analysis to more modern methods like as algorithmic trading and options trading. Despite the fact that every trading strategy has its own set of advantages and disadvantages, there is no trading method that is universally applicable. Discovering a trading strategy or set of techniques that corresponds with your trading style, level of comfort with risk, and financial objectives is of the utmost importance. Experiment with a variety of various methods, adjust your strategy to the conditions of the market, and continually improve it depending on the comments you receive and the experiences you have.

The mindset of a trader is an important factor in determining their level of success in the market. It is vital to cultivate a mindset that is both disciplined and resilient in order to be successful in conquering obstacles, keeping one's concentration, and recovering from failures. Fear, greed, and overconfidence are examples of emotions that can impair judgement and lead to mistakes that are expensive to remediate. You will be able to handle the ups and downs of trading with grace and composure if you cultivate emotional intelligence, practise mindfulness, and don't lose your grounding in reality.

As you move beyond the pages of this book and continue your adventure in trading, it is important to keep in mind that success in trading is not determined by gains or losses seen in the short term, but rather by your capacity to learn, adapt, and develop over the course of time. You should maintain your sense of wonder, your humility, and your dedication to your quest towards self-improvement and mastery. As you strive to become the greatest trader you can be, it is important to surround yourself with mentors, peers, and materials that will inspire and push you.

At this point, I would like to take this opportunity to convey my heartfelt appreciation to you, the reader, for accompanying me on this journey. My knowledge and thoughts have been shared with you, and it has been an honour and a privilege to do so. I hope that you have found this book to be interesting, useful, and empowering. It is important to keep in mind that the process of trading is not a running race but rather a marathon. If you have patience, perseverance, and desire, you will be able to realise your financial goals. I wish you the best of luck in both your investments and in life. I bid you farewell, and I hope that the markets continue to show you favour.

www.ingramcontent.com/pod-product-compliance
Lightning Source LLC
LaVergne TN
LVHW020432080526
838202LV00055B/5154